LET YOUR SPIRIT SOAR

WRITTEN & COMPILED BY: M.H. CLARK · DESIGNED BY: JESSICA PHOENIX

COMPENDIUM
live inspired.

◆◆◆◆◆◆◆◆◆◆

You have a gift to give. It doesn't take lots of time or extra money or concentrated effort, because that gift is a simple one, and you give it every day. That gift is your spirit—the brightest and truest part of you. You give of your spirit when you make time for delight, when you cherish yourself and the people you love, and when you see wonder in the everyday. You give of your spirit when you bring out the best in yourself, when you let yourself play, and when you revel in the present. And every time your spirit shows, you give a gift of brightness and warmth. You illuminate the world. So give that gift. Elevate your spirit. Turn your light on.

...everything in life responds
to the song of the heart.

ERNEST HOLMES

BE TRUE TO THE
BEST OF YOURSELF

...learn to seize your joy, for joy is always near.

JOHANN WOLFGANG VON GOETHE

There are only two ways to live your life. One is as though nothing is a miracle. The other is as though everything is a miracle.

ALBERT EINSTEIN

There is not enough darkness in
all the world to put out the light
of even one small candle.

ROBERT ALDEN

...be glad of life because it gives you
the chance to love and to work and
to play and to look up at the stars...

HENRY VAN DYKE

The spark divine dwells in thee: let it grow.

ELLA WHEELER WILCOX

COUNT ON
UNEXPECTED
BLESSINGS

...the miraculous is always nearby and
wonders shall never, ever cease.

ROBERT FULGHUM

You can dance anywhere,
even if only in your heart.

UNKNOWN

There are no ordinary moments.

DAN MILLMAN

Possibilities for adventure, beauty,
and goodness are all around you.
And happiness is in your hands.

VIRGINIA MILLER

...you are the window through which you must see the world.

GEORGE BERNARD SHAW

Do something brilliant every day.

ROGER VON OECH

You are only one thought
away from a good feeling.

SHEILA KRYSTAL

WAKE WITH WONDER

Every day is a fresh beginning...
every morn is the world made new...

SUSAN COOLIDGE

My favorite word is YES!

LENORE KANDEL

LET YOUR
DREAMS
BE YOUR
GUIDE

It is difficult to say what is impossible,
for the dream of yesterday is the hope
of today and the reality of tomorrow.

ROBERT H. GODDARD

...a light heart lives long.

WILLIAM SHAKESPEARE

△ △ △ △ △

If you can walk, you can dance.
If you can talk, you can sing.

ZIMBABWEAN PROVERB

Where there is love and inspiration,
I don't think you can go wrong.

ELLA FITZGERALD

In this moment, there is plenty of time. In this moment, you are precisely as you should be. In this moment, there is infinite potential.

VICTORIA MORAN

LOVE THE PERSON YOU ARE TODAY

Whatever you're ready for is ready for you.

MARK VICTOR HANSEN

Each day comes bearing its own gifts.
Untie the ribbons.

RUTH ANN SCHABACKER

I still get wildly enthusiastic about little
things...I play with leaves. I skip down
the street and run against the wind.

LEO BUSCAGLIA

Life is best experienced with a sense
of awe, wonder and discovery. Go about
life with a child's curiosity. (The universe
is more spectacular than you can imagine...)

TOM GREGORY

SEE THINGS
AGAIN
FOR THE
FIRST
TIME

Let the winds of enthusiasm sweep through you. Live today with gusto.

DALE CARNEGIE

Delight in the little things.

RUDYARD KIPLING

I have adopted the technique of living
life from miracle to miracle.

ARTHUR RUBINSTEIN

Your spark can become a flame
and change everything.

E.D. NIXON

BELIEVE

And above all, watch with glittering eyes the whole world around you because the greatest secrets are always hidden in the most unlikely places. Those who don't believe in magic will never find it.

ROALD DAHL

People are like stained-glass windows.
They sparkle and shine when the sun is out,
but when the darkness sets in, their true beauty
is revealed only if there is a light from within.

ELISABETH KÜBLER-ROSS

WITH SPECIAL THANKS TO THE ENTIRE COMPENDIUM FAMILY.

CREDITS:

Written by: M.H. Clark

Designed by: Jessica Phoenix

Edited by: Robin Lofstrom

Creative Direction by: Sarah Forster

ISBN: 978-1-935414-60-5